The Poetry of Me

Izzy Wagner

Published by Izzy Wagner, 2024.

THE POETRY OF ME

First edition. May 5, 2024.

ISBN: 979-8224963171

Written by Izzy Wagner.

Table of Contents

Dedication

To the seeker of stars, the dreamer of dawns, and the weaver of words,In the echoes of your verses, you've painted the sky with hues unseen, sculpted galaxies from syllables, and breathed life into the silence of pages. This collection stands as a testament to your unwavering commitment to uncovering the universe within and without, capturing fleeting moments with the grace of a wandering soul.To all those I've hurt, I offer my sincerest apologies. My actions may have caused pain, and for that, I am truly sorry. I recognize the impact of my words and deeds, and I humbly ask for your forgiveness.To everyone reading this, thank you. Your presence here, whether in curiosity or camaraderie, is deeply appreciated. Your engagement with these words gives them meaning beyond mere ink on paper or pixels on a screen.To all who have helped me along this journey, thank you. Your support, guidance, and encouragement have been invaluable. You've illuminated the path forward and lifted me up when I faltered.And to all who have hurt me, thank you. Your challenges have been lessons in disguise, shaping me into who I am today. Through adversity, I've discovered resilience, empathy, and the strength to persevere.May these poems serve as guiding constellations for those who wander in the labyrinth of existence, offering solace in solitude, courage in chaos, and whispers of truth in the cacophony of life's symphony.With boundless admiration and deepest gratitude

I've never enlisted AI to craft a single word of my writing. Not a syllable. Nada. Zip. I've no intention of ever outsourcing any aspect of my storytelling to AI, not even for eradicating typos. I cherish my typos.

Does this imply I doubt AI's potential to surpass me in storytelling someday? Absolutely not. It's bound to outdo me just like it does in chess. It might even master my style, complete with my colloquialisms like "gonna" and "trounce." Fine by me. Let the challenge commence.

What I bring to readers (admittedly, it's not much) is simply myself. I'm the analogue entity. The scratchy vinyl record. The worn-out sock with a hole in the heel. There's a humanity in my flaws, and that's my only bargaining chip. While many readers may flock to flawless books penned by ingenious AI in the centuries ahead, there will always be just one source for stories crafted by the flesh-and-blood me.

The Poetry of Me: A Personal Anthology

By: Izzy Wagner

Dedication Page

To the seeker of stars, the dreamer of dawns, and the weaver of words,

In the echoes of your verses, you've painted the sky with hues unseen, sculpted galaxies from syllables, and breathed life into the silence of pages. This collection stands as a testament to your unwavering commitment to uncovering the universe within and without, capturing fleeting moments with the grace of a wandering soul.

To all those I've hurt, I offer my sincerest apologies. My actions may have caused pain, and for that, I am truly sorry. I recognize the impact of my words and deeds, and I humbly ask for your forgiveness.

To everyone reading this, thank you. Your presence here, whether in curiosity or camaraderie, is deeply appreciated. Your engagement with these words gives them meaning beyond mere ink on paper or pixels on a screen.

To all who have helped me along this journey, thank you. Your support, guidance, and encouragement have been invaluable. You've illuminated the path forward and lifted me up when I faltered.

And to all who have hurt me, thank you. Your challenges have been lessons in disguise, shaping me into who I am today. Through adversity, I've discovered resilience, empathy, and the strength to persevere.

May these poems serve as guiding constellations for those who wander in the labyrinth of existence, offering solace in solitude, courage in chaos, and whispers of truth in the cacophony of life's symphony.

With boundless admiration and deepest gratitude

Foster Care

A Glimpse

In the future's embrace, foster care shall bloom,
    A sanctuary of hope, dispelling gloom.
    Where every child finds solace, love's tender kiss,
    In a world where no one's left to reminisce.
    Gone are the days of neglect and despair,
    In the arms of compassion, all burdens we share.
    A tapestry woven with threads of care,
    Each soul nurtured, each heart made aware.
    For every child, a guiding light,
    Through the darkest of hours, shining bright.
    No longer adrift in the storms of fate,
    But anchored in love, a destined state.
    With voices heard and dreams unfurled,
    In the embrace of a kinder world.
    Foster care's future, a beacon's glow,
    Guiding each child to flourish and grow.
    With open arms and hearts so wide,
    We'll walk beside them, side by side.
    For in the future of foster care,
    Lies a promise of love beyond compare.

Warriors

In a world of shifting shadows, Where whispers dance on fragile air, In the arms of uncertainty, we stand, Bound by threads of hope and care. Through the labyrinth of life, we roam, Seeking solace in the unknown, In the corridors of fleeting homes, Our hearts, resilient, find their own. Each door a portal to a new chapter, Each face a mirror of our own, In the tapestry of transient love, We weave our tales, though often alone. Yet in the echoes of our silent dreams, In the spaces between the tears we shed, We find the strength to rise again, To paint our tomorrows with colors, not yet bled.
For in the arms of adversity, We learn the language of resilience, In the embrace of strangers turned kin, We find the essence of our brilliance. So let the world define us not by circumstance, But by the courage that beats within, For in the tapestry of our journey, We are more than just where we've been.
In the foster care system's embrace, We're warriors, poets, and dreamers, true, Navigating storms with hearts ablaze, For in our stories lies the world anew.

Struggles

In the shadows where sunlight's scarce,
Echoes whisper of hearts laid bare,
In the maze of makeshift homes they roam,
Children lost, yet not alone.
Beneath the cloak of broken dreams,
Where silence reigns and darkness teems,
They carry burdens not their own,
In the foster care system's groan.
With every shuffle, every sigh,
A plea unheard, a tear to dry,
They navigate a world unkind,
Seeking solace they struggle to find.
In the dance of bureaucracy's might,
Innocence fades into the night,
Bound by chains of neglect's sting,
They yearn for love's gentle wing.
Yet amidst the chaos, a flicker glows,
A beacon of hope where empathy flows,
For in the hearts of those who dare,
Lies the power to heal, to repair.
So let us weave a tapestry bright,
Of compassion, of love, and of light,
For every child who's lost their way,
In the foster care system's sway.
Let us stand as guardians, strong and true,
To nurture, protect, and see them through,
For in their eyes, we'll come to see,
The resilience of humanity.

A House Not A Home

Foster Care the home of the lost,
Where broken hearts and dreams are tossed.
A place of love for the unloved,
Where hope is found and fears are shoved.
For those who have no place to go,
Foster Care becomes their only home.
They come from different walks of life,
With stories of struggle, pain, and strife.
But in this home, they find a new start,
A family that mends their broken heart.
They find love, support, and care,
In the arms of those who are there.
Foster parents with open hearts,
Provide a safe haven, a brand new start.
They give these children a sense of belonging,
And help them heal from the wounds of longing.
In Foster Care, they learn to trust,
To let go of the past and adjust.
They find a sense of stability,
In this temporary family.
But sometimes, the road is rough,
As old wounds can be tough.
But with love and patience, they heal,
And learn to believe in a brighter future that's real.
Foster Care, a place of love and grace,
Where every child finds their rightful place.
No longer lost, no longer alone,
They finally have a place to call their own.
So let us open our hearts and doors,
And welcome these children with open arms.

In Foster Care, lives are changed,
And beautiful stories of hope are arranged.

Parental Problems

Our parents, they raised us with care
    Guiding us through life's winding stair
    Their love so pure, their hearts so big
    Their presence always made us feel so snug
    But as we grow older and wiser
    Their expectations become much higher
    Their words, their actions, their every move
    Suddenly becomes a mental health groove
    They want the best for us, we know
    But sometimes it feels like an endless show
    Of trying to please and meet their standards
    Leaving us feeling mentally battered
    Their words can cut like a sharp knife
    Leaving us questioning our worth and life
    Their constant nagging and criticism
    Can lead to a mental health cataclysm
    We try to explain, to make them see
    But they refuse to understand, can't you see?
    That their actions have consequences
    On our mental health, it leaves dents
    We love them dearly, that's for sure
    But sometimes we need a mental health cure
    From the pressure, the expectations they set
    It's time for us to break free from this net
    So, parents, please listen to us
    Don't cause our mental health to be a fuss
    We need your love, your support, your care
    Not the burden of expectations to bear
    Let's work together, hand in hand
    To build a healthy mental health land

Where love and understanding reign
And our mental health doesn't have to strain
Our parents, they are our guiding light
But sometimes they can cause a mental health plight
Let's communicate, let's be open and kind
And create a world where mental health can shine.

Is It Love?

A love that seemed so pure and true
Turned into a nightmare, a horror to go through
He said he loved me, promised to protect
But his touch, his actions, left me wrecked
I trusted him with all my heart
But he tore it apart, shattered it apart
He took what was mine, without my consent
Left me broken, left me bent
I could never have imagined this pain
From someone I loved, it felt so insane
I thought he was my safe place, my rock
But he turned out to be a predator, a shock
My body, once mine, now feels tainted
His hands, his words, they left me painted
With bruises and scars, both inside and out
I couldn't escape, I was filled with doubt
Why did he do this, what did I do wrong?
Was it my fault, did I lead him on?
Questions that haunt me, every single day
As I struggle to find my voice, to find my way
But I refuse to be silenced, to be a victim
I will speak out, I will not be hidden
I am more than just a statistic, a number
I am a survivor, I will not slumber
To all the other girls, who have been through the same
You are not alone, you are not to blame
Together we'll fight, we'll break the silence
And put an end to this violence
No one deserves to be violated
No one should ever feel so degraded

Let's stand together, let our voices be heard
And show the world, that we will not be deterred
So to my ex-boyfriend, who thought he could control
I am stronger now, I have found my soul
You may have taken my body, but not my spirit
I am a warrior, and I will not fear it.

Change

New faces, new names

        In a system that never stays the same

                A new social worker, another change

But will they listen, or just rearrange?

        Years in care, different faces each time

                Trying to connect, but it feels like a climb

Opening up, sharing my fears

        But will this new worker hear my tears?

                I thought they were here to help

But it feels like I'm just a number on a shelf

        They come and go, in and out of my life

                And I'm left wondering, will they cause more strife?

I try to explain, to make them understand

        But they seem too busy, too caught up in their own plan

                My voice gets lost, in the chaos of their mind

And I'm left feeling alone, left behind

        I wish they could see, the pain within me

                But they just nod, and say they'll see

They don't hear the silent screams

        Or the shattered pieces of my dreams

                I am more than a case file

More than just a child in denial

        I have a voice, a heart, a soul

                But to them,

I'm just another story to be told

        I long for someone who will truly listen

                Someone who will see past the system

Someone who will hear my cries

        And help me heal, before another goodbye

                But for now, I'll just keep on trying

Hoping that one day, I'll find someone who's willing
To listen, to understand, to truly care
Until then, I'll just hold on to my despair

The Rushing Rain

In the steamy veil of dawn's embrace,
Where water cascades in a hurried race,
There lies a tale of fleeting showers,
Bound by time's relentless powers.
A symphony of droplets dance and sway,
As seconds tick, they swiftly obey.
Each splash a note in this ephemeral song,
As moments slip, they swiftly move along.
With every droplet, a fleeting dream,
In the shower's embrace, a silent scream,
For time's cruel hand knows no refrain,
In the realm of the rushing rain.
Oh, to linger longer, to let time stand still,
But duty calls, with a persistent will.
So we savor each drop, in this timed ballet,
Before reality sweeps our dreams away.
In the sanctuary of the shower's spray,
We find solace in this brief delay,
Knowing that though time may swiftly flee,
In these moments, we are truly free.
So let the water fall, let the minutes fly,
In the rhythm of the rain, we'll defy
The constraints of time, if only for an hour,
In the sacred space of the rushing shower.

Wanderlust's Refuge

In transient whispers, secrets told,
    A nomad's tale, both brave and bold.
    Each dawn, a new horizon calls,
    Through valleys deep and towering walls.
    With knapsacks packed and spirits high,
    We bid farewell to yesteryears' sigh.
    Through winding roads and starlit skies,
    We chase the dream that never dies.
    In hidden corners, we find our rest,
    Beneath the moon's soft, gentle crest.
    With every step, a story we weave,
    In search of solace, we believe.
    Though shadows linger, cast in doubt,
    Our wanderlust will not be routed out.
    For in the journey, we find our peace,
    Wherever wanderlust's whispers cease.
    So hand in hand, we'll roam the lands,
    Through shifting sands and rocky strands.
    In every moment, together we'll stand,
    In wanderlust's refuge, hand in hand.

Unheard Echoes

In the chambers of my soul, a silent scream,
Whispers of trauma, a broken dream.
Yet when I share, the words I weave,
Fall upon deaf ears, they don't believe.
Like shadows dancing in the night,
My truth obscured, out of sight.
Each tear that falls, a silent plea,
Lost in the void of disbelief's decree.
I paint my pain with words so clear,
But doubt and skepticism draw near.
They question the validity of my tale,
As if my suffering were a mere veil.
But within these wounds lies a truth profound,
Echoes of anguish, a haunting sound.
Though my voice may tremble, it rings true,
In the depths of my being, my trauma grew.
I am not a myth, nor a fiction spun,
My story, my scars, they are not undone.
For in the crucible of adversity, I stand,
A testament to resilience, hand in hand.
So, listen closely, if you dare,
To the whispers of my despair.
For in the silence, a strength unfurls,
Amidst the echoes of an unheard world.

Mending Hearts, Finding Light

In the quiet corridors of steel and stone,
Where solitude and shadows are my own,
Amidst the sterile scent of antiseptic air,
I find myself, a tender soul laid bare.
A journey marked by twists and turns,
In foster care, my spirit yearns,
For roots of love, for wings to soar,
Yet in this place, I seek for more.
Within these walls, where whispers hide,
I confront the demons deep inside,
Mental landscapes, tangled and vast,
But in the struggle, resilience is amassed.
Through the haze of doubt and fear,
I find a glimmer, small but clear,
A thread of hope in the darkest night,
Guiding me toward the morning light.
Though storms may rage and winds may howl,
I cling to faith, I make my vow,
To rise above the depths of despair,
And find the strength to mend and repair.
For in the intersection of pain and grace,
I forge my path, I find my place,
And though the journey may be long,
I'll emerge resilient, brave, and strong.
So let the echoes of my resilience ring,
In the halls where broken spirits sing,
For in this moment, I am free,
To write my story, to simply be.

Right's Rediscovered

In shadows cast by doubt's dark shroud,
A foster youth, unversed, unbowed,
In labyrinths where rights are veiled,
A quest for light, the heart assailed.
Unfamiliar paths, they wind and twist,
Through laws obscure, through the mist,
In the realm where justice strains,
Where clarity eludes, and doubt remains.
A tapestry of statutes weaved,
In language arcane, hopes deceived,
Yet in the soul, a spark ignites,
A yearning for truths, for guiding lights.
Though cast adrift in legal seas,
With rights obscured, like autumn leaves,
Strength emerges, a quiet might,
To claim the day, to seek what's right.
For in the depths, a strength resides,
In every beat where hope abides,
With courage bold, the unknown braves,
And wisdom's path, the heart engraves.
So, foster youth, amidst the haze,
Know your worth, in myriad ways,
For rights may hide, but never fade,
In your journey's stride, they'll find their shade.
Through knowledge sought, through voices raised,
In unity, the barricades,
Shall crumble down, and truth shall soar,
Foster youth, your rights restore.

Tomorrow's Echoes

In the cradle of uncertainty, I sway,
A transient soul, in the foster's way.
Tomorrow's echoes whisper tales untold,
In the tender grasp of a future's hold.
From fleeting homes to transient bonds,
In this labyrinth of life, my spirit responds.
A nomad amidst shifting sands,
I seek solace in destiny's hands.
Dreams unfurl like petals in bloom,
Yet, shadows loom in the impending gloom.
Will I find refuge in the arms of fate,
Or wander aimlessly through life's gate?
But hope, a beacon, steadfast and true,
Guides me through the haze, a resolute view.
For in the heart of every fleeting night,
Dawns the promise of a new daylight.
I am not defined by the past I've borne,
Nor shackled by the fears I've worn.
In the tapestry of time, I weave my own thread,
A symphony of resilience, where dreams are fed.
So let the future unfold, a canvas divine,
With hues of promise, in every line.
For in the heart of this foster child's plea,
Lies the courage to embrace what will be

Letters

To Dad

Dad thinks you are the problem
    Everything that goes wrong
    Every mistake, every mishap
    He puts the blame on you, all along
    You try to explain, to make him see
    That you are not the source of strife
    But he shuts you out, refuses to believe
    And pushes you away in his anger and strife
    He wants nothing to do with you
    His love and acceptance, it seems, has died
    You try to reach out, to bridge the gap
    But he turns his back, leaving you to cry
    You wonder what went wrong
    Why he sees you as the cause
    You try to be the best you can be
    But he only sees your flaws
    Dad, can't you see
    I am your child, just trying to find my way
    I need your love, your guidance, your support
    But you push me away, day after day
    You say I am the problem
    But I am just a reflection of you
    Your hurt, your pain, your unresolved issues
    It's not me, it's what you refuse to work through
    I will always love you, no matter what
    Even though you push me away
    I hope one day you will open your heart
    And see that I am not the enemy, in any way
    So, Dad, I'll keep trying
    To break through this barrier you've built

I'll keep showing you love and understanding
Hoping one day, our relationship will be rebuilt.

To My Younger Self

Dear younger me, so full of grace,
In memories' hall, I see your face.
Forgive me, for the trials we bore,
For the wounds we suffered, sore.
In innocence, you danced and played,
Unaware of shadows, fears arrayed.
I let you stumble, I let you fall,
But from those depths, we still stand tall.
The storms we weathered, fierce and wild,
Left scars upon the inner child.
I should have shielded you from harm,
Wrapped you safe within my arm.
Through tears and doubts, we found our way,
Learning lessons day by day.
But oh, the pain we could have spared,
If only I had truly cared.
So here I stand, with words sincere,
To wipe away the lingering tear.
I'm sorry, dear one, for what you went through,
I'll hold you close, I promise you.
Let's journey forward, hand in hand,
Embracing dreams, together we'll stand.
For though the past may cast its shade,
In love and healing, let us wade.
Forgive me, younger self, I pray,
For the moments lost along the way.
But know this now, and know it well,
In my heart, you'll forever dwell.

Thank You

My dear grandparents, so full of love

    You took me in, an angel from above

        My parents, unable to give me care

But you opened your arms, without a single dare

    You welcomed me with open hearts

        Nurturing me from the very start

With every kiss and every hug

    You showed me that I was never a burden or a bug

        With your words of wisdom and gentle touch

You taught me things that I needed so much

    From tying my shoes to riding a bike

        You were always there, without a single strike

Through thick and thin, you stood by my side

    With unwavering love, you became my guide

        In your warm embrace, I found my solace

No matter what, you never showed a trace

    Of regret or doubt for taking me in

        To you, I wasn't just another kin

But a precious gift, a blessing in disguise

    And for that, I'll be forever grateful, no lies

        You showed me the beauty of life

Through all the struggles and the strife

    You taught me to never give up hope

        And always find ways to cope

With your love and patience, you shaped me

    Into the person that I was meant to be

        You gave me the foundations to thrive

And taught me to always strive

    For my dreams and my future

        No obstacle was ever too obscure

And now, as I look back
      I see that my life was never off track
            Because of you, my dear grandparents
I am standing tall, unbreakable like cement
      You took me in and raised me as your own
         And for that, my love for you has only grown
So thank you, for being my guiding light
      For showing me the path that's right
        My dear grandparents, you mean the world to me
And in your loving arms, I'll always be free.

I'm Sorry

Our friendship once was strong and pure
We laughed and cried, we were so sure
That nothing could ever come between
The bond we had, the love we'd seen
But then one day, you had to go
To a new place, a new life to know
I smiled and hugged you, wished you well
But deep inside, my heart did swell
For I knew things would never be the same
Our daily talks, our inside jokes, our silly games
All would fade into memory
As you moved on, away from me
I tried to keep in touch, to stay connected
But our friendship slowly, silently rejected
The distance between us grew too wide
And slowly, our friendship slowly died
I watched as you made new friends
And my heart ached, I couldn't pretend
That I wasn't hurt, that I didn't care
But you were gone, and I was left with despair
And then one day, I heard the news
You had found someone, someone new
A new best friend, it stung like a knife
And I couldn't help but feel the strife
For you had moved on, left me behind
And now our friendship, I couldn't find
You were happy, but I was alone
And our friendship, now just a stepping stone
I wish you well, I really do
But know that my heart is torn in two

My best friend, now just a distant memory
As we go our separate ways, you and me.

Forgiveness in Bloom

In the garden of my memories, tangled vines of pain,
I once blamed you, dear mother, for the scars that remain.
Your footsteps faltered on life's uneven path,
Struggling beneath the weight of shadows that swathed.
In youth's naive gaze, I failed to comprehend,
The battles you fought, the demons you couldn't fend.
Through tear-streaked nights and silent screams,
Your heart, besieged by turbulent dreams.
Forgive me, for I couldn't see beyond my own dismay,
For every harsh word, for every bitter display.
You were a canvas, painted with hues of despair,
Yet beneath the layers, a soul worn but rare.
Mental storms raged, casting shadows long,
Yet through the tempest, your love stood strong.
In your fractured embrace, I found solace deep,
A bond unbroken, a treasure to keep.
Today, as I stand on the shores of hindsight clear,
I extend my hand, shedding the weight of yesteryear.
In the garden of forgiveness, blooms of healing rise,
As we embrace the truth beneath cerulean skies.
Mother, I offer my sincerest apology,
For the wounds inflicted in my blindness, I plea.
May our hearts intertwine, in love's gentle sway,
As we walk together, towards a brighter day.

Apologies Unspoken

In the whispering silence of regret, I find my voice,
A melody of sorry, a symphony of choice.
For in the tangled threads of love, I dared to weave,
A pattern not meant for me to conceive.
To my dear friend, in shadows of my own making,
I come bearing words, a heart heavy, aching.
I trespassed in the garden of your affection,
Unwittingly sowing seeds of misdirection.
Forgive me, for I overstepped my bounds,
In the dance of emotions, I tripped, confounds.
A spectator I should have remained, a distant witness,
Instead, I grasped, I interfered, I caused distress.
Your love, a sacred sanctuary, I invaded,
With intentions pure, yet actions shaded.
Blinded by concern, I stumbled in the dark,
Unaware of the wounds I inflicted, stark.
I apologize for the wounds I couldn't foresee,
For the pain I caused, for the discord, the plea.
Let time be the mender of fractures deep,
As I humbly retreat, in contrition, I steep.
May our friendship, weathered but not broken,
Rise above this storm, with words unspoken.
For in the realm of forgiveness, may we find peace,
And from this moment, let grievances cease.

Shadows of Uncertainty

In shadows cast by our past's gentle sway,
I find myself adrift in dim dismay.
What unseen error did my steps betray,
To lose the light of friendship's gentle ray?
Was it a word misspoken, left unsaid,
Or silence, where I should have warmly tread?
In tangled webs of thoughts, my mind is led,
Seeking solace in apologies unread.
The tapestry we wove, now frayed and torn,
Each thread of trust unravelled, left forlorn.
With heavy heart, I mourn what once was born,
And pray forgiveness may be newly sworn.
Though words may falter, stumbling in their flight,
And understanding hides in veils of night,
Know that my remorse burns fierce and bright,
In hopes that reconciliation might.
So let us mend what time has rent apart,
Rekindle flames of friendship in our heart.
Forgiveness, like a balm, may heal the smart,
And from the shadows, let us gently depart.

Whispers of Apology

In the silence of the night, I hear
Echoes of your laughter, so near
Yet distant, like a fading dream
In the passing of a moonbeam.
I'm sorry for the times I've gone,
Leaving you to face the dawn
Alone, with burdens hard to bear,
Without a whisper of my care.
In moments when I chose to roam,
Leaving you to build a home
Of memories without my part,
I've wounded with an absent heart.
Forgive me for the tears unshed,
For the words I left unsaid.
In the rush to chase my own desires,
I neglected to stoke our shared fires.
But know, dear siblings, in my soul,
Your presence fills an empty hole.
Though distance kept us far apart,
You've always dwelled within my heart.
So here I stand with words sincere,
Seeking solace, drawing near.
Let this poem be my embrace,
A token of love, in this space.

Unrequited Echoes

In the quiet depths where silence dwells,
Amidst the shadows where loneliness swells,
There lies a heart, weary and worn,
A soul ensnared, tangled and torn.
To you, dear one, whom I cannot reach,
Whose essence eludes my faltering speech,
In the mirror's gaze, I see your face,
A reflection of grace, a timeless embrace.
Yet distance veils what could have been,
A love unclaimed, a dream unseen,
For in the depths of my own abyss,
I find the echo of your gentle kiss.
Oh, how I long to hold you near,
To whisper words you'll never hear,
To cherish you with tender care,
But alas, you remain beyond my prayer.
You are the star that guides my night,
The song that fills my soul with light,
But I am but a fleeting shadow,
A wanderer in this endless meadow.
Though I may never touch your heart,
Know that you've been there from the start,
For in the depths of my own soul,
Your presence lingers, making me whole.
So let this letter be my plea,
A testament to the love in me,
Though I may never truly be enough,
I'll cherish you, dear self, through all life's rough.
With every beat of this weary heart,
I'll hold you close, never to depart,

For in the end, what truly matters,
Is the love we find within ourselves, in all its splendors.

Scar's of Strength

In the echoes of time, where memories reside,
I find my younger self, steadfast by my side.
Through trials and tempests, we journeyed as one,
A dance with darkness, yet under the sun.
Oh, younger self, with courage untamed,
In the heart of adversity, you remained.
Through storms that threatened to tear us apart,
You held on fiercely, with unwavering heart.
For every tear shed in the dead of night,
For every battle fought, for every plight,
I thank you, dear younger self, for your grace,
For enduring the pain, for finding your place.
In the tapestry of life, woven with care,
Your resilience shines, beyond compare.
Though scars may linger, they tell a tale true,
Of strength and endurance, embodied in you.
So here's to you, my younger self, so brave,
For weathering the storms, for rising from the grave.
In gratitude, I stand, for all that we've gained,
For the wisdom forged, for the lessons attained.
Through the labyrinth of time, hand in hand we roam,
Grateful for the journey, grateful for home.
Thank you, dear younger self, for the pain we've known,
For it sculpted us into the seeds that were sown.

A Tribute to My Ex's

In the room where it happened, we shared our highs and lows,
But now it's time to thank you, before this chapter closes.
Though love may fade and dreams may bend,
Our journey together, I won't pretend.
To my ex's, I owe a debt,
For the lessons learned, I won't forget.
In the melody of our past, I find my rhyme,
Thank you for the memories, for our time.
From helpless to satisfied, we danced our way through strife,
In your eyes, I saw the story of my life.
Though the world turned upside down, we stood tall,
Through heartache and laughter, we gave it our all.
To my ex's, I owe a debt,
For the lessons learned, I won't forget.
In the melody of our past, I find my rhyme,
Thank you for the memories, for our time.
In the quiet of the night, I reflect,
On the love we shared, the respect.
Though our paths diverge, I'll cherish the line,
That connects our hearts, for all of time.
To my ex's, I owe a debt,
For the lessons learned, I won't forget.
In the melody of our past, I find my rhyme,
Thank you for the memories, for our time.
So here's to you, in this final verse,
For the love we shared, for better or worse.
Though our story ends, a new one will start,
Thank you, my ex's, you'll always hold a part.

A Beacon In The Storm

In the tempest of life, where shadows loom,
You appeared, a beacon, dispelling gloom.
With empathy as your compass, you gently guide,
Through tumultuous seas, you're by my side.
In the tapestry of chaos, you weave a thread,
Of hope and resilience, where fears are shed.
Your words, like soothing balm, heal every wound,
In your presence, solace and comfort are found.
When the weight of the world becomes too much to bear,
You offer a sanctuary, a haven of care.
With patience as your virtue, you listen, you hear,
Each whispered concern, each silent tear.
Your actions speak volumes, louder than words,
In your compassion, the voiceless are heard.
You champion the cause of those in need,
A true advocate, in thought and in deed.
So, here's a heartfelt token, a humble tribute,
To the unwavering support you contribute.
For being the light in my darkest night,
I'm forever grateful, with all my might.

Healing

Constrained Melodies

In the heart of silence, echoes dwell,
Where freedom's whispers faintly swell.
Within the walls of a group home's keep,
Lies a realm where liberties weep.
Forbidden, the dance of youthful feet,
To tap out rhythms on floors concrete.
No skipping stones in the nearby stream,
Nor chasing dreams through moonlit gleam.
The laughter stifled, the joy suppressed,
In a realm where rules are firmly dressed.
Each flicker of rebellion quelled,
In corridors where hushed secrets held.
No wandering beyond the gates,
No serenades beneath starry fates.
Bound by regulations, chained by decree,
In this realm where autonomy's not free.
Yet in the shadows, hope still gleams,
A quiet rebellion, a spark that teems.
For within each soul, a fire resides,
Yearning to break from these confides.
So let us pen our tales of flight,
In clandestine ink, under shroud of night.
For though the rules may tightly bind,
The spirit within refuses to be confined.
In the hush of dusk, let us conspire,
To ignite the flames of our desire.
For even in darkness, stars still gleam,
And freedom's song is but a dream away, it seems.

Starting to Heal

Healing your inner child
is like tending to a fragile flower
nurturing and gentle
with each passing hour
It's understanding the wounds
that were once left untold
and holding them with love
as they slowly unfold
It's wiping away tears
that have been held for so long
and replacing them with laughter
like a beautiful song
It's embracing the innocence
that was taken away
and reminding your inner child
that it's okay to play
It's giving yourself permission
to let go of the pain
and finding the strength
to love yourself again
Healing your inner child
is a journey of self-discovery
a process of healing
and uncovering your true beauty
It's learning to forgive
those who have caused you harm
and finding peace within
like a soothing balm
It's reclaiming your power
and standing tall and strong

knowing that you are worthy
and have been all along
So take your inner child's hand
and lead them towards the light
for healing begins within
and it's a beautiful sight.

Phoenix Rising

In shadows deep, where scars still bleed,
I tread the path of pain's cruel creed.
Beneath the weight of shattered dreams,
I sought the light in silent screams.
Through days of dusk and nights of woe,
I wandered lost, with nowhere to go.
In echoes of your words unkind,
I found a darkness in my mind.
But from the ashes of despair,
A flicker of hope lingered there.
With tender hands and whispered grace,
I learned to find my rightful place.
Like the phoenix, I rose anew,
From embers of what once I knew.
With every tear that I have shed,
I've stitched my wounds, healed what was dead.
No longer chained to yester pain,
I dance in freedom's sweet refrain.
For in the depths, I found my might,
And emerged from the darkest night.
So let the scars become my art,
Each line a tale of a mended heart.
For in the healing, I have found,
A strength that once was tightly bound.
To those who caused my spirit harm,
I release you now, with no alarm.
For I have grown, I have forgiven,
And in that, my soul has risen.
So here I stand, in love's embrace,
A testament to time and grace.

With every step, I claim my flight,
A phoenix rising from the night.

The Artisan of Healing

In shadows deep, where silence thrums,
A journey starts, where no foot drums.
No guide, no hand to light the way,
Just whispers faint in dark of day.
In solitude, the soul does mend,
With threads of courage, it does tend.
No crutch, no brace, no aiding hand,
Just will and strength to make a stand.
Through valleys low and mountains high,
The path of healing winds and sighs.
No map to trace, no signs to read,
Just faith to plant the soul's brave seed.
Each tear that falls, each scar that bleeds,
Becomes a canvas for new deeds.
No brush, no paint, no artist's gaze,
Just time and grace in healing's maze.
The broken pieces slowly bind,
With whispers of the heart entwined.
No song, no verse, no poet's pen,
Just quiet strength that lives within.
So rise, oh soul, in silent might,
Embrace the journey, dark or bright.
No cradle, no shelter, no soft bed,
Just raw resolve to heal, instead.

A Daughter's Forgiveness

In shadows deep, where secrets lie,
    A daughter's heart learns to defy.
    Where wounds are deep, and tears oft shed,
    Forgiveness blooms in hues of red.
    Through tempests fierce, where anger swells,
    A daughter's soul breaks free from spells.
    To release the grip of bitterness' hold,
    And find in forgiveness, a story untold.
    For fathers stumble, as mortals do,
    Their struggles hidden, their burdens too.
    Yet in their frailty, love still resides,
    In forgiveness, bridges span divides.
    Though echoes linger of words unkind,
    Forgiveness whispers, a gentle wind.
    For in the depths of a wounded soul,
    Lies the strength to let forgiveness take control.
    So let forgiveness guide your weary heart,
    In the darkest hour, where shadows part.
    For in the act of letting go and forgiving,
    A daughter finds solace, a new beginning.

Embers of Empathy

In the dance of shadows and light,
Forgiveness blooms, a delicate sight.
Beneath the moon's forgiving gaze,
I pen these words, a healing phase.
Step sisters, in your veils of deceit,
Gaslighting whispers, cunning and discreet.
Yet, in my heart, I find the grace
To forgive, to let go, to embrace.
Your words, like daggers, pierced the air,
But I choose compassion, a tender care.
For in your depths, I see the pain,
The insecurity, the fear's domain.
Though you sought to dim my inner light,
I rise, resilient, in the still of night.
For in forgiveness, there's a power untold,
A liberation, a warmth, a story yet unfold.
So here I stand, amidst the fray,
With forgiveness as my guiding ray.
Step sisters dear, I release the strife,
And in its place, I offer life.
Life abundant, with love's refrain,
Where understanding heals the pain.
Together, we'll mend what once was torn,
And in forgiveness, new bonds are born.
So let us walk, hand in hand,
Across the shores of forgiveness' land.
For in its grace, we find our way,
And in its light, we choose to stay.

Of Scars and Stars

In the quiet of the dawn's embrace,
Where shadows fade and light finds space,
There blooms a tale of inner grace,
Of healing from a hidden chase.
From depths where darkness once held sway,
A heart emerges, finds its way,
Through scars that tell of yesterday,
Yet yearn for peace, a brighter day.
Each wound a whisper, etched in skin,
A testament of where we've been,
But healing starts from deep within,
Where courage finds its voice to win.
In tender hands, the broken mend,
With patience as their faithful friend,
They nurture wounds, they softly tend,
And in their care, the hurt will end.
For strength is found in every scar,
A symbol of how brave we are,
To face the pain, to heal, to mar,
And still emerge, a shining star.
So let the tears, like rain, descend,
And let the broken hearts amend,
For in the journey, we transcend,
And find our way to peace, to mend.

Reclamation

In the silent caverns of the night,
Where shadows dance and fears take flight,
There blooms a whisper, soft and tender,
A beacon of hope, a path to render.
From shattered pieces, a soul may rise,
As phoenix from ashes, towards azure skies,
For in the depths of darkest pain,
Lies strength to mend, to rise again.
Through the echoes of a harrowing past,
A journey unfolds, though shadows cast,
With each step forward, reclaiming ground,
A symphony of resilience, profound.
Scars may linger, etched upon the skin,
Yet within the heart, a spark within,
A flame of courage, fierce and true,
Guiding the wounded to start anew.
With gentle hands and tender grace,
Embracing the self, in sacred space,
Healing whispers, a soothing balm,
Offer solace, a tranquil calm.
For every tear shed in the night,
Holds within it, a glimmering light,
A testament to the strength within,
A testament to the journey to begin.
So let the healing waters flow,
From depths within, let healing grow,
For in the heart's relentless beat,
Lies the melody of triumph sweet.
In the tapestry of scars and pain,
A story of resilience, it shall reign,

For from the ashes, a spirit soars,
In the dance of healing, forevermore.

Tools of Grace

In the quiet hum of dawn's embrace,
Where shadows dance with morning grace,
There lies a sanctum, a sacred space,
Where tools of healing find their place.
In the tender touch of a painter's brush,
Strokes of color, emotions rush,
Canvas whispers, a silent hush,
Capturing moments, dreams to crush.
A potter's wheel spins tales untold,
Clay molded, stories unfold,
Hands shaping beauty, as hearts behold,
In earth's embrace, dreams take hold.
A poet's pen, a mighty sword,
Ink spills like rivers, thoughts poured,
Words weaving tapestries, adored,
Healing wounds, by truth implored.
Gentle hands wield surgeon's knife,
Cutting through darkness, bringing life,
Stitching souls, amid the strife,
Guiding through the darkest strife.
But beyond these tangible things we see,
Lie the tools within, pure and free,
Love's embrace, empathy's decree,
Kindness and compassion, eternally.
So let us cherish these tools of grace,
In the journey of life, in every place,
For they heal the wounds, without a trace,
And fill our souls with endless grace.

Grace's Tapestry

In the silent whispers of the night,
When shadows dance and fears take flight,
I found a solace, pure and clear,
A guiding hand, always near.
Through valleys deep and mountains high,
Beneath the vast and starlit sky,
God's gentle touch, a soothing balm,
Has healed the wounds, brought calm.
In moments of despair and pain,
When tears fell like the pouring rain,
A divine embrace, tender and true,
Whispered, "I am here for you."
Through trials fierce and tempests wild,
With every step, like a trusting child,
I've felt the presence, strong and kind,
Guiding heart and soothing mind.
In seasons of joy and laughter's embrace,
In every challenge I bravely face,
God's love endures, unwavering and bright,
Guiding me through the darkest night.
So here I stand, healed and whole,
A testament to the boundless soul,
For through the years, God's love did steer,
And stitched my wounds with threads of cheer.
In the tapestry of life's design,
God's grace and mercy ever shine,
For every scar, a story told,
Of how God's love has made me bold.

Whispers of Mending

In shadows deep, where silence reigns,
Lie memories cloaked in veils of pain.
Unspoken wounds, they quietly weep,
In the chambers of my soul, they sleep.
But hark, there comes a gentle breeze,
Through whispered words, it seeks to ease.
It whispers secrets, soft and kind,
Of healing paths I long to find.
Through labyrinthine corridors,
Where echoes of past battles soar,
I tread with care, yet undeterred,
For in the dark, my light's conferred.
With each step forward, scars unfurl,
Like petals in a dawn-lit swirl.
The wounds, once raw, now start to mend,
As whispers of hope softly ascend.
I learn to embrace the broken parts,
To weave them into newfound arts.
For in the tapestry of my being,
Lies the beauty of my unseen healing.
No longer bound by silence's chain,
I rise from depths of hidden pain.
With every word that finds its way,
I reclaim my strength, come what may.
So let the whispers turn to song,
A melody where I belong.
For in the healing, I am free,
To embrace the truth inside of me.

Blossoming Beyond Time

In the cradle of dawn, where innocence fades,
A child thrust into realms, where maturity cascades.
Forced to dance with shadows, in the dimming light,
Yet within this crucible, a spirit takes flight.
Beneath the weight of burdens, too heavy to bear,
A soul yearns for laughter, for dreams to repair.
Through the labyrinth of sorrow, and the tempest's roar,
A heart finds resilience, on unfamiliar shore.
In the garden of adversity, where roses bloom,
Each thorn a reminder, of a childhood's gloom.
Yet, from the ashes of youth, a phoenix arises,
With wings unfurled, and hope that mesmerizes.
Through tears of yesterday, and scars that adorn,
A journey unfolds, where new beginnings are born.
With each step forward, a healing embrace,
Embracing the beauty, in rediscovered grace.
So let the wounds mend, in the gentle embrace of time,
As the echoes of resilience, in every heart chime.
For though the innocence lost may never return,
In the garden of healing, new lessons we learn.

About the Author

Izzy Wagner was 15 when she first experienced the Foster Care System. She was in one of the hardest moments of her life when her parents agreed it was best. As an adult, Izzy has realized that she should have been in the system a lot earlier than 15 but also realizes that she got lucky to be fostered by family. Izzy Wagner works on one of the Minnesota State Boards, with four different non-profits across Minnesota, and one nation wide as a Youth with Lived Experience. Izzy Wagner has published a couple of articles with The Imprint as well.

"I wrote this book to remind anyone who is struggling, whether it be with the Foster Care System or in general, that there is a light at the end of the tunnel. I remember that darkest point in my life and want to be someone's reason to keep going when they can't find anything else to keep them here. Just a little bit of hope can go along way" Izzy Wagner states.